SCHOLASTIC

Reading Response Scrapbooking Activities

by Michael Gravois

New York • Toronto • London • Auckland • Sydney
Mexico City • New Delhi • Hong Kong • Buenos Aires

Teaching *Resources*

DEDICATION

For those who live in memories—
especially Joe

Cover design by Jason Robinson
Interior design by Michael Gravois
Interior illustrations by Teresa Anderko and Jim Palmer
Photo Credits: Page 5: (rulers, pencil, and scissors) Photodisc via SODA; (compass) Artville via SODA; (crayons) John Lei via SODA; (stickers) Artville via SODA.
Pages 8 and 23: Ken Karp/SODA.

ISBN-13 978-0-439-54893-9
ISBN-10 0-439-54893-4

1 2 3 4 5 6 7 8 9 10   40   13 12 11 10 09 08 07

TABLE OF CONTENTS

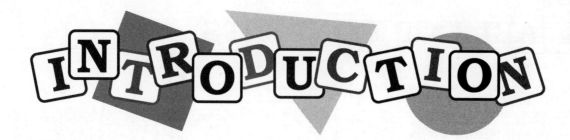

INTRODUCTION

Making scrapbooks as a way of preserving family memories is one of the most popular home crafts in the country. Scrapbookers combine photographs, journaling, and careful placement of art elements to create original family treasures that transport the reader down memory lane.

Now the art of scrapbooking is heading off to school! In every curricular area, scrapbooking gives students the chance to use their organizational, writing, and artistic skills while recording their learning in a fun, hands-on way. Scrapbooking invites students to conceptualize an idea, organize their thoughts, and get their hands and minds actively involved in expressing these thoughts three-dimensionally. You'll find your reluctant writers wondering how they can best report the information they've learned in the space available. And your artistically-challenged students will develop techniques for expressing their ideas visually.

Perhaps the most powerful way scrapbooking can be applied as a learning tool is through reading response activities. Scrapbooking provides an open-ended, interpretive medium through which students can synthesize their learning and generate visual and linguistic responses to fiction and nonfiction books of all genres. The flexibility of these activities addresses the different intelligences found within every classroom by allowing students the freedom to use their individual strengths to find connections between the text and their own lives.

This book has been designed to help you blend the joy of scrapbooking with its educational benefits. It is not just a how-to book, but also a resource for inspiration. To get started, look at the ideas presented in this book, review the teacher tips that accompany each project, and let your imagination run wild. The possibilities are endless.

MATERIALS & TOOLS

GETTING STARTED

There are many materials that can be used for scrapbooking projects in the classroom, but some basic tools are necessities. To help build your inventory, ask each student to bring in the following materials at the beginning of the school year:

- a roll of tape
- several glue sticks
- a good pair of scissors
- a packet of colored pencils
- a packet of thin, colored markers

Set up a scrapbooking station in your classroom where a few students can work at a time. Have students clean up and restock the workspace after each use. They can help keep the station stocked by contributing extra stickers, holiday cards, stencils, markers, and so on.

Throughout the years, add other scrapbooking tools to your inventory. Before you know it, your students will be producing incredible scrapbook projects that reflect the wide variety of subjects they've been studying.

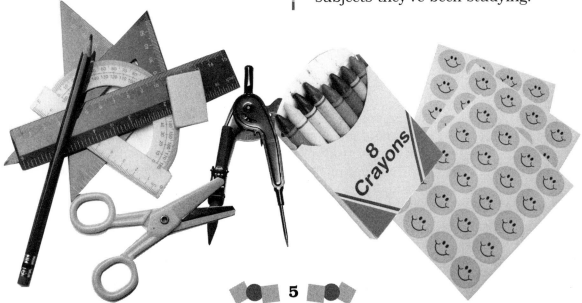

LIST OF MATERIALS

ADHESIVES—There are many different kinds of adhesives suitable for scrapbooking (glue sticks, liquid glue, spray glue, glue pens, rubber cement, two-sided tape), each with their strengths and weaknesses. But for overall ease and neatness, glue sticks are the most versatile for classroom use.

CLIP ART—Clip and use images to dress up the scrapbook page. Clip art is available in books, on Web sites, or on computer programs. Students can find clip art arranged by theme to help them with specific projects. *See pages 16–19 for clip art samples.*

COLOR WHEEL—Encourage students to consult a color wheel to help them choose colors that will enhance their scrapbook pages. *Conduct the activity on page 10 so that each student can have a personal color wheel.*

COMPASS—A compass is a handy tool that helps you make circles and arcs. Students can cut photographs into circular shapes and add rounded designs to scrapbook pages.

COMPUTER/INTERNET ACCESS—There is no research tool more powerful in the classroom than a computer. A world of information is available with the click of a button. Invite students to find information on the topics they're studying, download clip art and images to enhance their projects, and access Web sites devoted to scrapbooking.

CRAFT KNIFE—Craft knives with replaceable blades make it easy to cut intricate designs and heavy-stock paper. However, because of the sharp blade, you might want to do this type of cutting for your students.

CRAFT PUNCHES—Create an interesting border around a scrapbook page with craft punches. These devices feature a wide variety of shapes and sizes, from ovals and squares to footprints and palm trees. Students can also use the confetti shapes they punch out to decorate the page. Another type of craft punch is a corner rounder, whose name says it all—it rounds the corners of scrapbooking materials, primarily photographs. Some corner punches, known as photo corners, cut a slot in the four corners of a mat, allowing a photograph to be mounted without the use of glue.

DIE CUTS—These precut shapes can be bought individually or in themed packets. You can find them in assorted colors and designs, but if you can't find the color you want, simply use the die-cut design as a template and trace it onto the desired color or pattern of paper and cut it out. You—or your school—can also buy a die cutting machine to make enough patterns for everyone in your class. Use the negative portions of the die cuts as interesting frames.

DIGITAL CAMERA—In addition to the benefit of allowing students to take photographs that can be added to their scrapbook pages, digital cameras provide opportunities for your class to engage in creative dramatics. Students can pose as historical figures for a scrapbook on Colonial America; they can act like scientists for a page devoted to microbiology; or they can create a scene that illustrates the climax of a novel they just read.

DIMENSIONAL GLUE—Dimensional glue, or puffy paint, comes in a rainbow of colors, in a variety of finishes—glossy, glittered, metallic, and so on. Use dimensional glue to create borders, outline titles, and add pizzazz to scrapbooks.

ERASERS—Traditional erasers are fine for classroom use, but kneaded erasers are softer and less abrasive.

LETTERING BOOKLETS—There are many books available that feature easy-to-draw lettering styles that students can use for titles and headlines. *See pages 11–15 for more ideas on lettering.*

LIGHT BOX—A light box is an acrylic box that has a light bulb inside it. You can use it to transfer a clip art design directly to the scrapbook page. Place the clip art on top of the light box and your scrapbook page on top of the clip art. The light inside the box allows you to trace the art. You can achieve the same result by holding the paper up to a sunlit window in the classroom.

MAGAZINES AND GREETING CARDS—Ask students to bring in old magazines and greeting cards from which images and photographs can be clipped to use on scrapbook pages.

PAINTS—Use watercolors and tempera paints to create interesting textures and backgrounds for your scrapbook pages.

PAPER—Paper is an essential component of scrapbooking and comes in a variety of colors, textures, patterns, and weights. Provide a wide assortment of paper choices for the students to use—construction paper, copier paper, stationery, decorative paper, cardstock, and so on. Wrapping paper provides a variety of designs that students can cut out. Ask students to bring interesting sheets of wrapping paper to class.

PAPER CUTTER—Though not a necessity, a paper cutter is a luxury in the classroom. It helps you trim paper to a specified size, creating straight cuts and square corners.

PENS, PENCILS, AND MARKERS—Like paper, writing instruments are essential to scrapbooking. In addition to the standard pens, pencils, and markers, ask your students to bring in gel pens, calligraphy pens, metallic pens, and other novelty pens they own. Crayons provide another creative option, allowing students to make rubbings for their scrapbook.

PHOTO CORNERS—Use these little self-adhesive corners to hold photographs. First put them on the corners of the photo, and then stick them to the scrapbook page.

PLASTIC BAGS—Use small self-sealing bags to hold three-dimensional objects (flowers, sand, trinkets, and so on). Tape or glue the bags to the page.

RUBBER STAMPS AND INK PADS— Stamping is a craft that rivals scrapbooking in popularity. Students can find rubber stamps to fit nearly any theme, and ink pads come in a multitude of vibrant colors. What a fun way to decorate a page!

RULERS—Every student should have a traditional straight-edged ruler for measuring and drawing straight lines. But now novelty-edged rulers are available, allowing students to create ornamental borders and fancy lines.

SCISSORS—By the fourth grade, most students' hands are too big for the small, cheap, metal scissors that many schools provide. (You know the ones I'm talking about.) If your school doesn't provide adequate scissors for your class, ask each student to buy a pair of high-quality straight-edged scissors for classroom use. Throughout the years, you can also add decorative-edged scissors to your scrapbooking station. These fun scissors cut distinctive edges on pages and photographs—wavy, scalloped, zigzagged, rippled. It will be hard to choose just one pair.

STENCILS AND TEMPLATES—Use stencils and templates to trace patterns onto paper and photographs so they can be cut into a variety of shapes. Cookie cutters work well as stencils. Templates that feature different styles of lettering make it easy to create bold, clean titles for scrapbook pages.

STICKERS—Collect stickers that you get through book clubs and teacher stores. Encourage students to bring in extra stickers they have. Each year your inventory will grow until you have a nice selection for students to use. Stickers are a quick, fun way to add color and life to a scrapbook.

THREE-HOLE PUNCH—If your students are constructing a scrapbook that is several pages long, a three-hole punch provides a quick binding solution. Simply punch the holes in the left edge (or top) of each page and bind them together with three strands of yarn.

TRIANGLE—A clear, plastic, right-angle triangle makes it easy to draw straight, parallel lines and align graphic elements on the page.

THE COLOR WHEEL

The color wheel is a helpful tool for choosing colors that complement each other and enhance the scrapbook page. Color selection can add vibrancy and movement to a page, establish an overall mood, or tie graphic elements on the page together.

The color wheel is comprised of three *primary colors* (red, blue, and yellow), three *secondary colors* (purple, green, and orange) which are combinations of the primary colors, and six *tertiary colors* (red-orange, yellow-orange, yellow-green, blue-green, blue-violet, and red-violet) which are combinations of primary and secondary colors.

Colors that are directly opposite each other on the color wheel (such as blue and orange) are called *complimentary colors.* Complimentary colors create a lot of vibrancy and movement. They tend to stand out from each other. Use complimentary colors when you want graphic elements to jump out at the viewer. Just be careful not to let the use of complimentary colors upstage the content of the page.

Choose colors that are directly next to each other on the color wheel (such as blue and blue-green) to create a sense of harmony on the page. These types of colors are called *analogous colors.* Analogous colors can add atmosphere and mood to your project. These colors are often grouped into *cool colors* (blue, green, and purple) and *warm colors* (red, yellow, and orange). It is said that warm colors seem to advance toward the viewer, while cool colors seem to recede. Warm colors appear to be more vibrant, while cool colors seem more peaceful.

The use of color can help reinforce the theme of the page. For example, blue and blue-green would be ideal for a page that focuses on ocean life; red, white, and blue are an obvious choice for a page on the American Revolution. What colors do each of the four seasons bring to mind? What colors do you associate with outer space? With your favorite sports team? With different holidays? Consider bright colors, pastels, earth tones, neutrals, and various shades of one color when choosing the best palette for a project.

Have students use colored pencils or markers to complete the color wheel activity sheet on page 10. Remind them to keep it handy to help them with color selections for future projects.

COLOR WHEEL ACTIVITY SHEET

Name _____ Date _____

Use colored pencils or markers to color the corresponding sections on the color wheel.

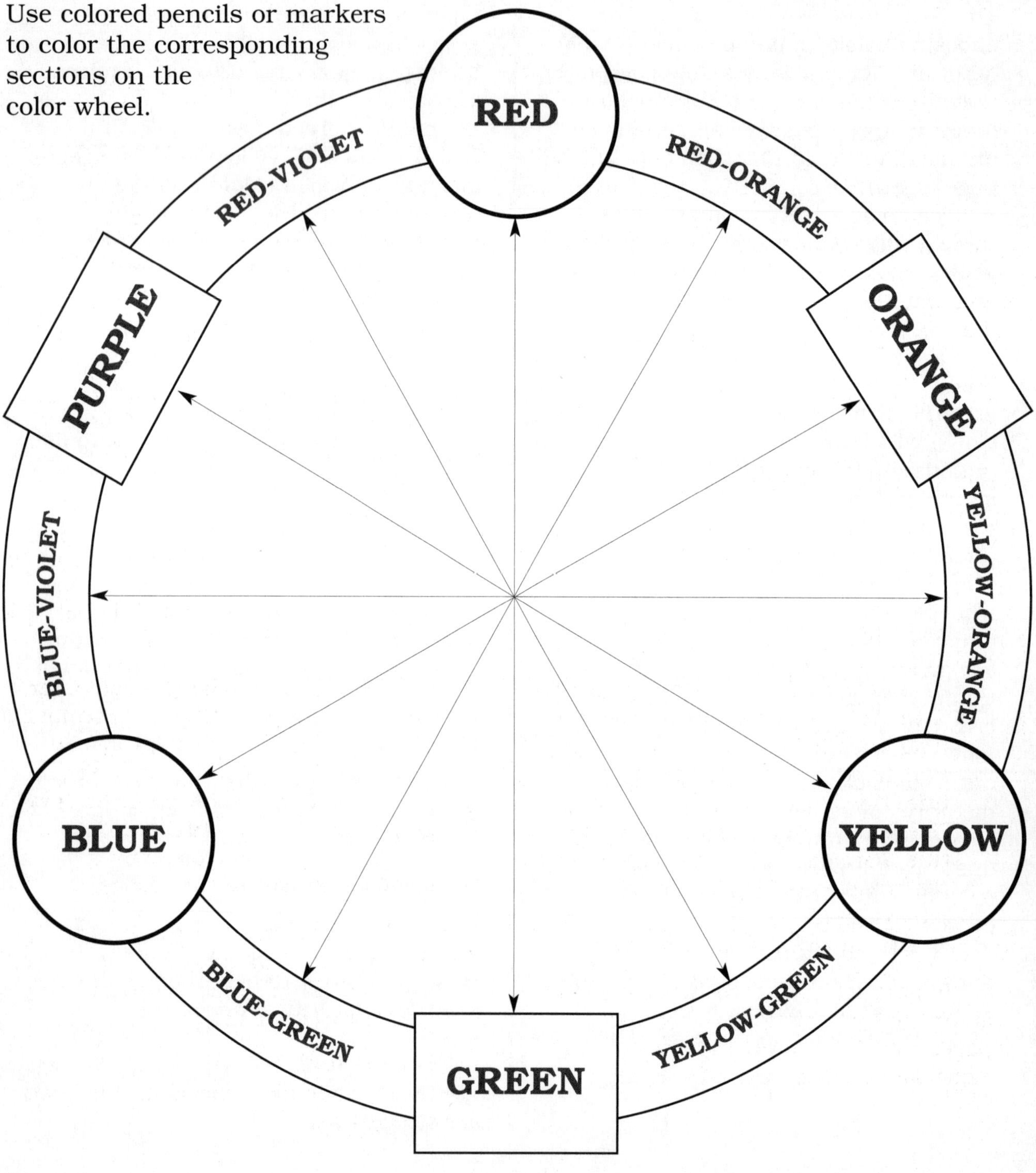

RED

RED-VIOLET

RED-ORANGE

PURPLE

ORANGE

YELLOW-ORANGE

BLUE-VIOLET

BLUE

YELLOW

BLUE-GREEN

YELLOW-GREEN

GREEN

When planning a scrapbook page, it is important to consider the amount of space needed for the title. A creatively lettered title can really add punch to the layout. It will be the first thing that catches the reader's eye. So be sure to have a wide assortment of pens, pencils, and markers available for the students to use. Model the steps below to help students with the placement of a title:

1. Choose a title for a page and count the number of letters and spaces it contains.
2. Divide that number in half to find the middle of the title.
3. Then use a pencil to make a mark on the page where you want the center of the title to appear.
4. Use a ruler to draw pencil lines marking the top and bottom of the title's height.
5. In pencil, write the middle letter of the title at the center point, continuing backwards to the first letter.
6. Finish lettering the last half of the title. It will now be centered.
7. Use pens or markers to make the title more decorative. *Check out the sample lettering styles on pages 12–15.*
8. Erase any stray pencil marks.

In addition to the freehand lettering styles that students can copy from pages 12–15, encourage them to experiment using their own ideas.

Students can also try the following techniques:

STENCILS—Stencils are a great way to create clear, bold letters. But students can still add their own personal touch to the lettering. After tracing the letters students can color or decorate them any way they'd like.

STICKERS—A wide selection of alphabet styles and sizes are available in sticker form. You can also find many styles that are themed—animal prints, holiday-inspired, futuristic, and so on.

RUBBER STAMPS—Everyone loves using rubber stamps. Inexpensive sets that feature the full alphabet can be found at most craft stores.

COMPUTER FONTS—Using a computer, students can print titles in a banner form, or they can print out individual letters and glue them to the page separately. Show students how to tilt the letters a little (like those in the title on this page) to add some movement to the design.

DIE CUTS—Die cuts are precut letters that students can glue onto the page individually. Die cuts come in a wide variety of colors and shapes.

Be sure to look at the different titles used in the sample projects in this book for other ideas.

DECORATIVE FONTS

DRAW THE LETTER. A   ADD A LARGE DOT AT EACH POINT. A

A a   B b   C c   D d

E e   F f   G g   H h

I i   J j   K k   L l

M m   N n   O o   P p

Q q   R r   S s   T t

U u   V v   W w

X x   Y y   Z z

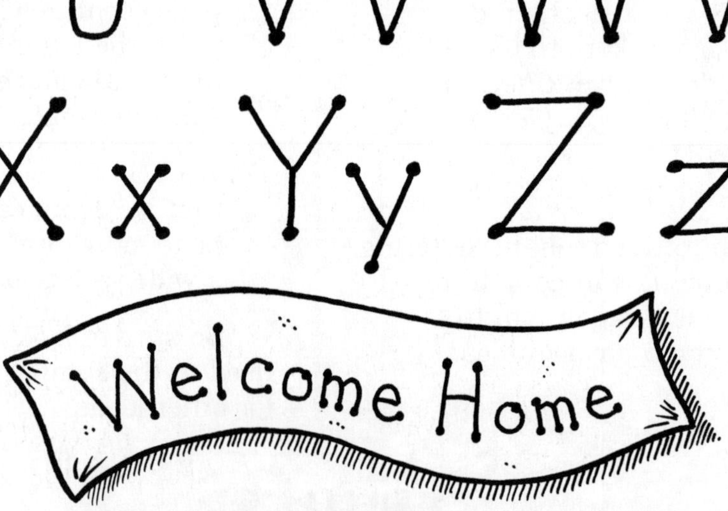

Welcome Home

DECORATIVE FONTS

DRAW A LETTER. A   ADD TWO LINES TO ONE SIDE. ⫻A

Aa Bb Cc Dd
Ee Ff Gg Hh
Ii Jj Kk Ll
Mm Nn Oo
Pp Qq Rr Ss
Tt Uu Vv Ww
Xx Yy Zz

SCHOOL DAYS

DECORATIVE FONTS

DRAW THE LETTER. A ADD A LINE TO EITHER SIDE. A MAYBE FILL IN WITH A DESIGN. A

Aa Bb Cc Dd

Ee Ff Gg Hh

Ii Jj Kk Ll

Mm Nn Oo

Pp Qq Rr Ss

Tt Uu Vv Ww

Xx Yy Zz

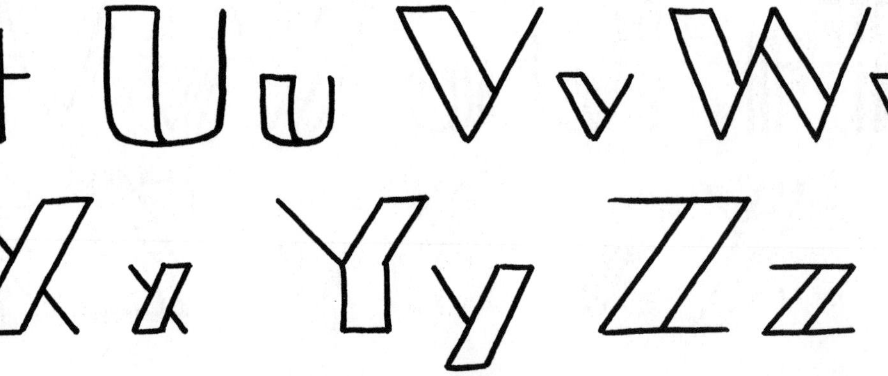

AUTUMN FEST

DECORATIVE FONTS

DRAW AN OPEN-FACE LETTER.  CREATE A DIFFERENT DESIGN FOR EACH LETTER. A-Z

WINTER

CLIP ART

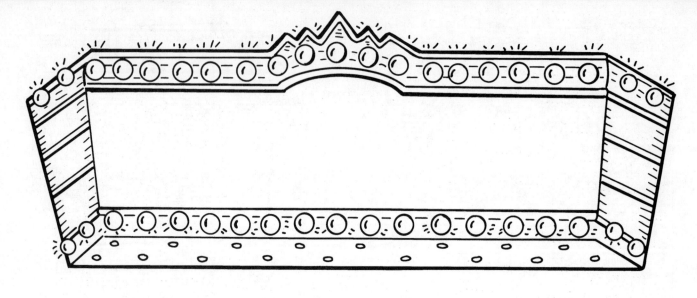

JOURNALING

Scrapbooks are not just collections of objects and mementos; they're also journals in which remembrances and observations are recorded. In fact, the written word—or journaling—is often more important than the photograph or the souvenir. Journaling is what truly makes the scrapbook a reflection of its creator.

Sometimes a journal entry describes the object or photo included on the scrapbook page, and sometimes it describes how the journalist felt when the object was found or when the photo was taken. Journaling can be written in fragmented sentences or in complete paragraphs. It can include original poetry or the words of a favorite poet. The words can appear in a column or surround the outer edge of the page. Invite students to be creative! Try different things!

Journaling in one's own handwriting makes the page seem more personal, but if there is a lot of information to convey, a word processor is a great tool.

It is sometimes beneficial for students to take the "Do, Learn, Feel" approach to journal writing—encourage them to talk about what they did, share something that they learned, and describe how they felt. This helps make the entries more detailed and interesting.

When journaling, use the "5 Ws and How" to help overcome writer's block.

WHO—Who does the object remind you of? Who is in the picture? Who was with you on the trip?

WHAT—What did you do? What was the mood like at the event? What is your favorite/ least favorite memory? What is the significance of the object?

WHEN—When was the picture taken? When did the event take place? When did you pick up this memento?

WHERE—Where did you get the souvenir? Where was the picture taken? Where else did you go?

WHY—Why did you save this object in particular? Why did this event take place?

HOW—How did you feel? How old were you? How much did it cost?

Students can use the Journaling Web on page 21 to help them brainstorm ideas about what to write.

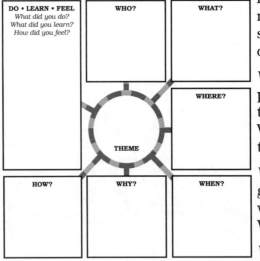

DO • LEARN • FEEL
What did you do?
What did you learn?
How did you feel?

WHO? — WHAT? — WHERE? — THEME — HOW? — WHY? — WHEN?

 JOURNALING WEB

Name _____ **Date** _____

Write the theme of the scrapbook page in the center circle. Brainstorm ideas that relate to the "Do, Learn, Feel" and "5 Ws and How" prompts. Use these ideas to help you write vivid journal entries on your page.

DO • LEARN • FEEL
What did you do?
What did you learn?
How did you feel?

WHO?

WHAT?

WHERE?

THEME

HOW?

WHY?

WHEN?

PROJECTS

Starting on page 30 are 18 scrapbooking ideas for the classroom. Use them as inspirations for developing scrapbooking projects that your students can create. Mix and match ideas from different projects or incorporate them into different subject areas. For example, the first project, How I Spent My Summer Vacation, could be adapted as a reading response assignment by having students create a similar scrapbook that features souvenirs from a trip that a character from a novel might have taken, or it could be used as the starting point for a nonfiction project where students create a scrapbook as if they'd taken the journey with Columbus to the New World. (Check out the grid, ADAPTING THE PROJECTS, on pages 26–29 for additional ideas.)

Begin each project with a brain-storming activity. After discussing the nature of the project, ask students to come up with a list of different items and objects they could include on their scrapbook page; each project lends itself to different kinds of items. Write the list on the board for students to refer to as they work on their project. A suggested list of items that could be included on scrapbook pages can be found below.

It is also a good idea to let students know exactly what is required of them. You can do this by creating a requirement sheet and a rubric that clearly outlines your expectations. A sample

SCRAPBOOK ITEMS

Advertisements	Coins	Magazine clippings	Quotes
Announcements	Definitions	Maps	Recipes
Awards	Drawings	Menus	Report cards
Bills	Dried leaves	Newspaper clippings	Resumes
Birth certificates	Family trees	Obituaries	Reviews
Brochures	Floorplans	Photographs	Rubbings
Bumper stickers	Greeting cards	Playbills	Sheet music
Business cards	Handprints	Poetry	Song lyrics
Calendar pages	Illustrations	Postcards	Thank-you notes
Cartoons	Invitations	Pressed flowers	Ticket stubs
Certificates	Letters	Programs	Travel guides

requirement sheet and rubric can be found on pages 24 and 25.

As an extension activity to build students' schema—or conceptual understanding—ask them to bring in family scrapbooks to share with the class. This is a great way for students to get to know each other, and the personal scrapbooks could inspire them to start ones of their own. The more students are exposed to the art of scrapbooking, the easier it will be for them to generate original ideas themselves.

Another great idea is to save the scrapbooking projects each student makes throughout the year and then bind the pages into a finished scrapbook that you can send home with students on the last day of school. Each scrapbook is a "snapshot" of the year the students spent with you, and they will become wonderful keepsakes for students to turn to in years ahead. Of course, doing this would dictate the basic foundation the students use to construct their scrapbook. The projects shown in this book use a variety of foundations: posterboard, boxes, tri-fold boards, cardboard, construction paper, and so on. If you want to compile the scrapbook projects into one bound book, students could use large sheets of construction paper as the foundation for each page.

CHARACTER SCRAPBOOK

This project will be a character study of the main character of your book and will take the form of a scrapbook. You are to create a scrapbook page as if it were put together by the main character.

SCRAPBOOK PAGE—The scrapbook page's background should reflect the main setting of the story, over which you will glue the other scrapbook elements listed below. The background should also include the character's name, the title of the book, the author's name, and your name. Be creative about how you incorporate each of these elements.

JOURNAL ENTRY—Write a journal entry from the main character's point of view that gives a summary of the book. The journal entry should be written in complete paragraphs and include a brief description of the main character, setting, major events, and conclusion.

PICTURES AND PHOTOGRAPHS—Five pictures or photographs should be included ("photos" can be drawn or cut out of magazines). Paste the pictures throughout the scrapbook and include an explanation that describes what is shown in each. They should illustrate each of the following:
- the main character in a scene from the book
- the character's family or friends
- the main character's major accomplishment
- the setting of the story
- a picture of your choice that relates back to the book

ADVICE COLUMN—Write a letter to an advice columnist from the main character's point of view that explains the main problem the character faces in the novel. Write another letter from the columnist's point of view that includes the solution to the problem as it happens in the story.

SOUVENIRS AND MEMENTOS—Draw, create, collect, or find at least six souvenirs that the main character would have put into the scrapbook. These objects should reflect events in the story or important aspects of your character. Include an explanation next to each object describing its significance.

DIARY ENTRY—Write a diary entry from the main character's point of view that reflects the main character's feelings about himself or herself at the beginning of the story. Write a second diary entry that describes how the character changed by the end of the story.

CHARACTER MINI-BOOK—Use the directions on page 65 to create a six-page mini-book that features an illustration and description of six characters in the story.

SPELLING, GRAMMAR, PUNCTUATION, NEATNESS—Make sure your spelling, grammar, and punctuation are correct and that the overall look of the scrapbook is creative and neat.

CHARACTER SCRAPBOOK RUBRIC

1. The scrapbook page includes the character's name, the title of the book, the author's name, and your name. It is creatively illustrated and reflects the character who created it.

    10   9   8   7   6   5   4   3   2   1   0

2. The journal entry is written in the first person, includes a summary of the book, and uses complete paragraphs.

    10   9   8   7   6   5   4   3   2   1   0

3. The pictures/photographs are creative and detailed. They illustrate the five required categories. A complete sentence describes each picture.

    10   9   8   7   6   5   4   3   2   1   0

4. The advice column describes the problem and solution in complete paragraphs. It is imaginative and descriptive.

    10   9   8   7   6   5   4   3   2   1   0

5. The souvenirs and mementos are creative, and they are representative of the character and the story. A complete sentence describes each object.

    10   9   8   7   6   5   4   3   2   1   0

6. The diary entry reflects the character's feelings about himself/herself, describes how the character changed throughout the story, and is written in the first person.

    10   9   8   7   6   5   4   3   2   1   0

7. The mini-book contains creative drawings of six main characters. The sentences about each character are accurate and descriptive.

    10   9   8   7   6   5   4   3   2   1   0

8. Grammar and sentence structure are correct (no fragments or run-on sentences; verb tenses are correct).

    10   9   8   7   6   5   4   3   2   1   0

9. Spelling and punctuation are correct.

    10   9   8   7   6   5   4   3   2   1   0

10. The overall look of the scrapbook is creative and neat. The layout is carefully planned.

    10   9   8   7   6   5   4   3   2   1   0

ADAPTING THE PROJECTS

PROJECT	MORE READING RESPONSE IDEAS
How I Spent My Summer Vacation p. 30	**Character Study**—Imagine how a character in a book would spend his or her summer vacation. **Culture Study**—Read about different cultures or celebrations. Create a scrapbook as if you took a vacation to the region you studied.
All About Me Scrapbooks p. 32	**Autobiographies**—Become familiar with the genre of autobiographies as you construct a scrapbook that focuses on your own strengths, history, and interests. **Hobbies**—Research a hobby that you'd like to explore in more depth. Create a scrapbook poster to illustrate what you've learned.
First & Last Days of School p. 34	**Character Development**—After reading the first chapter of a novel, create a scrapbook page from the point of view of the main character. Then create another page after finishing the novel that shows how the character changed over the course of the story. (You can construct a similar project in a notebook, adding a new page after each chapter.) **History**—Track the progress of a historical event, focusing on its origins and its aftermath.
ABC Scrapbooks p. 36	**Textbook Forecast**—Choose a letter of the alphabet (no two students should choose the same letter), and look through the indexes of your textbooks to get an idea of the various topics you'll be studying in the year ahead. Construct a scrapbook page that focuses on your letter. Present your "forecast" to the class.
Scrapbook Book Reports p. 38	**Story Elements Study**—Create a scrapbook that focuses on a specific story element—characters (protagonist, antagonist, or secondary characters), setting, plot, problem, or solution. **Genre Studies**—Read a book from a specific genre and create a scrapbook book report that highlights characteristics of the genre you chose and explains why this book falls into that category.

PROJECT	MORE READING RESPONSE IDEAS
Poetry Scrapbooks & Journals p. 40	**Poet Study**—Learn more about the artistic process and the people who write poetry. Choose a favorite poet, research him or her, and create a scrapbook devoted to this artist. Write a poem in the style of this poet; include a timeline of his or her life; recount things that inspired this person. What inspires you?
Daily Journal Scrapbooks p. 44	**Reading Response Journals**—Use the prompts on pages 45–46 as springboards for creating a reading response scrapbook. Brainstorm ways in which each of the prompts can take the form of a scrapbook entry. **Scrapbook Diaries**—Keeping a daily diary can provide an important outlet for processing life's trials and joys. Scrapbook diaries are even more important to the diarist because they include important mementos and keepsakes of life's journey.
Tri-Fold State Scrapbooks p. 48	**Exploring Settings**—Create a tri-fold scrapbook that focuses on the setting of a book, whether or not it's a real or fictional place. Include maps, postcards, photographs, directions, plane tickets, stamps, and so on.
Scrapbox Country Reports p. 50	**Prediction Boxes**—Fill a box with objects associated with a particular book the class is about to read. Pull out the objects one by one and ask the class to suggest ways in which each object will play a part in the story. Then read the book to see which predictions were accurate. **Celebrating Favorite Books**—Prepare a scrapbox book report that focuses on your favorite book. Give an oral presentation to the class, explaining the meaning of each object found in the box.
A Decade in Review p. 52	**Thematic Posters**—With a group of classmates, read different novels that all relate to a similar theme— bullying, coping with death, oppression, self-image, and so on. As a group, create a learning poster that illustrates what your group learned about the theme and features elements about how each book deals with the theme. **Nonfiction**—Read a nonfiction book about a specific time period and create a learning poster that focuses on fads, fashion, politics, people, and events described in the book.

PROJECT	MORE READING RESPONSE IDEAS
Desk Blotters of Famous People p. 54	**Author or Character Study**—What types of things might your favorite author keep on his desktop? What might you find on the desk of a literary character? **Social Studies**—Research a career you might like to pursue. Think about how you could use an object related to this field—such as a desk blotter, briefcase, easel, dashboard, music stand, artist's palette, clipboard, and so on—as the background for a scrapbook page.
Animal Habitat Posters p. 56	**A Change of Setting**—Divide a sheet of posterboard in half. On one side, create a scrapbook poster that focuses on the setting of a novel you read. On the other half, illustrate ways in which the story might have changed had the author chosen a distinctly different setting. **Scientific Reading**—Create a habitat poster that focuses on an environment related to a science topic you are studying. For example, what type of environment nurtures germs? What would you find on the surface of Venus? What animals live beneath the soil in your backyard?
Science Experiment Scrapbooks p. 58	**Exploring Science**—There are many books that focus on scientific theories related to a wide variety of topics. Choose a topic that interests you, research it, ask questions, develop a hypothesis, and then conduct an experiment to test your hypothesis. Visit your local library to find books filled with related activities.
The Art of Geometry p. 60	**Exploring Picture Books**—Read a picture book that focuses on geometry or math, such as *Grandfather Tang's Story* by Ann Tompert, *The Greedy Triangle* by Marilyn Burns, *G is for Googol: A Math Alphabet Book* by David M. Schwartz, or *The Math Curse* by Jon Sciezka. Create a scrapbook page based on the concepts expressed in the book you read. **Geometric Shapes in Art**—In nearly every "How to Draw" book, the first section focuses on breaking down objects and figures into basic geometric shapes. Read one of these books, and then create a scrapbook page that features shapes cut from construction paper that have been arranged as a still life. Use this working model to draw or paint a finished piece of art.

PROJECT	MORE READING RESPONSE IDEAS
Scrapbooking Graphs & Charts p. 62	**"Reading" Graphs**—What genre is the most popular in your school? Who read the most books over the summer? Which literary antagonist is the most evil? Conduct class and school surveys and record the data in a reading scrapbook.
The Wide World of Sports p. 64	**Political History**—Just as there are wins and losses in sporting events, there are victories and defeats in political battles. You can learn about the history of a society by studying significant elections. Read selections from a textbook, and create two scrapbook pages that feature political buttons, platforms, and biographical information about opposing candidates. **Biographies**—Rather than focusing on a specific sport, you could read the biography of a famous athlete. Construct a scrapbook that this person might have created. It could contain a birth certificate, awards and recognitions, newspaper articles, family photos, ticket stubs, letters from admirers, and other important objects.
Cereal Box Scrapbooks p. 66	**Story Elements**—Find a cube-shaped box. Cover the box with construction paper or bulletin board paper. On five of the sides, glue objects and sentences that focus on five major story elements, such as plot, character, setting, problem, and solution. On the sixth side, write the name of the novel, the author's name, and your name. **Book Covers**—Turn a cereal box into a large book—complete with front and back covers and a spine. Design a cover that represents the main idea of the book and a back cover that offers a synopsis of the book. Fill the cereal box with index cards that feature vocabulary words you learned when you read the book.
Bulletin Board Scrapbooks p. 68	**Sequencing**—[Teacher: Ask the class to read a novel. Next, divide a bulletin board into as many sections as there are chapters in the novel. Then divide the class into small groups. Assign a different chapter to each group and have them complete the activity.] Collect and create scrapbook elements that relate to your assigned chapter. Place your scrapbook pieces on the bulletin board in sequential order. Remember to include a synopsis of your chapter.

Summer afternoon—summer afternoon; to me those have always been the two most beautiful words in the English language.
—Edith Wharton

HOW I SPENT MY SUMMER VACATION

During the first days of school, ask students to construct a scrapbook page that features highlights from their summer vacation. This allows them to reconnect with each other, share fun experiences, and practice their public speaking skills in a safe, relaxed environment.

Students can include postcards, brochures, letters, bumper stickers, coins, tickets, maps, and other mementos on their scrapbook page. If they don't have actual materials from their holiday, they can construct or draw them.

Hidden Surprises
Surprise readers by placing pictures behind doors and windows, inviting them to "come on in."

Send a letter home before the school year starts explaining the project and asking students to collect things over the summer that could be included in the scrapbook. Also ask students to bring in old buttons, twine, ribbons, and beads that can be used in scrapbooking projects throughout the year. Store them in shoeboxes for easy access.

Backgrounds
Maps and brochures make interesting backgrounds for scrapbook projects. This background uses brochures from the Florida Welcoming Center.

TIP

If you want to include a lot of journaling on the scrapbook page, use a brass paper fastener to attach several pages together. This allows the reader to flip through the pages easily.

Secret Message Journaling

Highlight words within your journaling to create a secret message!

Carly's Daily Journal!

DAY ONE

Thanks to seven beautiful days of sunny weather, we enjoyed a fantastic trip to Florida this summer. On July 1st, **Mom and Dad** woke us up at 4:00 in the morning to get an early start—**for** the drive to Orland would take us twelve hours. We only made **a** couple of stops—for breakfast and lunch—but otherwise we drove straight through. We knew we were in for a great **vacation** when we arrived at the Grand Floridian and saw how spectacular it was. **I** quickly threw my things into my room and we headed to the Rainforest Cafe for dinner. Our waiter, **WILL**, was very funny and friendly. Then we saw the Electric Light Parade. I **never** saw so many lights! I went to bed knowing the coming days would make me **forget** my troubles and fill me with the magic of Disney!

Artistic Accents

Use discarded slide frames to create interesting accents for the page.

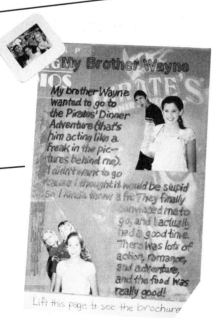

My Brother Wayne

My brother Wayne wanted to go to the Pirates' Dinner Adventure (that's him acting like a freak in the pictures behind me). I didn't want to go because I thought it would be stupid so I kinda threw a fit. They finally convinced me to go, and I actually had a good time. There was lots of action, romance, and adventure, and the food was really good!

Lift this page to see the brochure.

Tracing Paper

Consider writing journal entries or headlines on tracing paper, allowing the "ghost" of background images to appear from behind the writing.

FOCUS ON READING

Ask students to read brochures, travel guides, maps, and nonfiction books about the place they went on their summer vacation. If they didn't take a trip, they could study a place they would like to visit, or they could learn more about the city or town in which they live. Encourage students to share interesting things they learned with their classmates.

ALL ABOUT ME SCRAPBOOKS

Students will get to know each other better by creating "All About Me" pages that can be bound together into a class scrapbook. Add this special scrapbook to the classroom library for everyone to enjoy throughout the year. When the year ends, it will become a wonderful keepsake for you, reminding you of the extraordinary children who touched your life.

Family Trees

Teach students about genealogy by having them create a family tree. They can get very detailed with it, or they can limit it to their immediate family.

Using Photographs and Artwork

Place cropped photographs over hand-drawn backgrounds to create a whole new look.

FOCUS ON READING

Encourage students to learn more about their heroes by inviting them to read biographies and autobiographies of these influential people. Challenge students to write a list of goals and accomplishments for themselves so they can inspire others!

Top Ten Lists

Ask students to create a small booklet that lists their top ten favorite things in the world and their top ten least favorite things in the world. (Use top ten lists in any curricular area: top ten favorite inventions, sports, books, songs, states, and so on.)

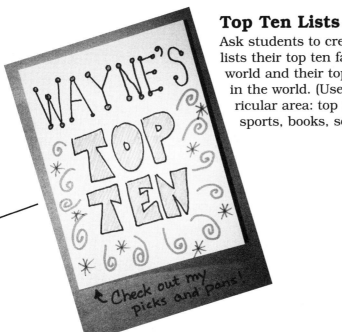

Self-Portraits

Teaching students how to draw self-portraits at the beginning of the school year lays a foundation for the understanding of facial anatomy. It will also help them draw better faces in future art projects. Use the "How To" at left for basic instructions.

HOW TO

Ask students to draw a self-portrait of themselves. Provide each student with a small hand-held mirror. (You might ask the art teacher to conduct this part of the project.)

1. Start by drawing an oval.

2. Divide the oval in half. The eyes and ears fall along this line, as shown.

3. Divide the lower half of the oval in half. The bottom of the nose touches this line.

4. Divide this lower quarter in half. The mouth falls along this line.

5. Add hair and other facial details, and then color the self-portrait.

FIRST & LAST DAYS OF SCHOOL

Self-evaluation is an important part of educational growth. It allows students to identify accomplishments, assess problem areas, and create a plan for future growth.

Nurture this skill in your students by having them track their goals and interests on the first day of school and then asking them to evaluate their progress at the end of the year.

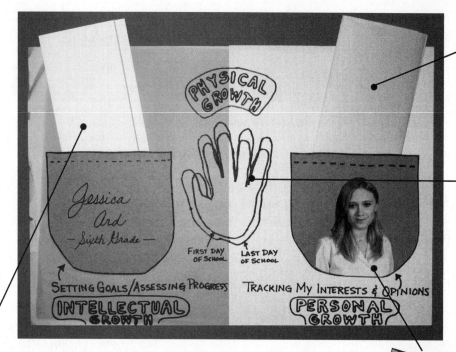

Intellectual Growth

On the first day of school, ask students to write a list of short-term and long-term goals they have for the year ahead. Return the list at the end of the year; on the back, have students discuss whether or not they met the goals they had set for themselves and describe what they can do in the future to better achieve their goals. Students can put their lists and responses into a pocket on their scrapbook page.

TIP

Save scrapbook pages in a place that gets little light so construction paper doesn't fade over the year (a large box works well). Or you can use acid-free paper that doesn't fade when exposed to light.

Pockets

Think of interesting ways to store letters and other printed materials, such as these pants pockets. To personalize the page, students can add school photos of themselves.

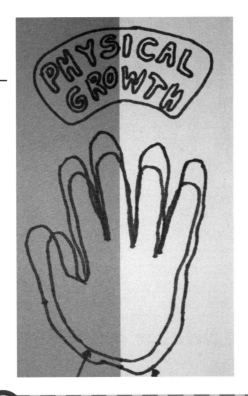

INTEREST INVENTORY

NAME: _Jessica Ard_   DATE: _October 17th_

Answer each question below and explain why you answered each question the way you did

1. If you could be anything in the world when you grow up, what would you want to be?
   A chef
2. If you could travel any place in the world, where would you go?
   San Francisco!
3. What is your favorite subject in school?
   Reading
4. What is your favorite hobby?
   I love to travel and knit.
5. What is your favorite TV show?
   I don't really watch television!
6. What is your favorite movie of all time?
   The Sound of Music
7. What is your favorite animal?
   My dog Bodecia
8. If you could be like any one great person, whom would you choose?
   Neil Armstrong because I would go into space
9. If you were given $1,000, what would you do with it?
   Travel
10. Name five things that you think are your strongest assets.
    Humor, smile, love of family, heart, esteem
11. If you could change one thing about yourself, what would it be?
    I want to dye my hair black.
12. Would you rather be very good looking, very talented, very smart, or very rich?
    Very rich, because I'm already smart!
13. What makes you happy?
    My family
14. Name five things that you are thankful for.
    Family, friends, Health, Happiness, Bodecia (my dog)

Personal Growth

Pass out copies of the interest inventory on page 70. Ask students to fill out the form and place it in a pocket on their scrapbook page. On the last day of school, pass out another copy of the inventory and ask them to fill it out. Students can insert this copy into the envelope, too, and then see how their interests and opinions have changed and developed over the year.

Physical Growth

Students can chart their physical growth by tracing their hand on the first day of school and then tracing it again in a different color on the last day of school.

TIP

A fun activity for the last week of school is to give your students all of the scrapbook pages they've made throughout the year and have them bind the pages together into a wonderful record of their year in your classroom.

FOCUS ON READING

Read the first chapter and the last chapter of a novel or the first and last pages of a short story. Ask students to predict events in the story that caused the main character to change. Then read the complete novel or short story to see if the predictions were accurate. Lead a follow-up discussion.

ABC SCRAPBOOKS

Like a scrapbook, each school year is filled with memories. Celebrate and document your successful year with oversized ABC scrapbooks.

ABC scrapbooks make a fun culminating activity for the end of the year.

Have students brainstorm things learned, places visited, and books that begin with their letters (see "M" below and "D" on page 37). You can also use ABC scrapbooks at the end of major units throughout the year.

HOW TO

1. Write the letters A–Z on the blackboard.

2. As a class, brainstorm all of the activities, units, field trips, assemblies, class novels, and events of the past year that begin with each letter.

3. Ask each student to select a different letter and create a scrapbook page featuring items related to that letter.

4. Collect the completed pages and alphabetize them.

5. Hang the pages in the hall for everyone to see. Create a banner that reads something like FIFTH GRADE MEMORIES.

6. After the last day of school, collect the pages and bind them into a book.

7. On the first day of the next school year, share the scrapbook with your new class. This will get them excited about all the things they will do in the coming year.

M Is for Molecules

What did your students read about in science this year? They can include small models, a page or two from daily logs, or photos of experiments to show off their science savvy.

M Is for Measurement

Encourage kids to include things they've learned in every subject on their scrapbook pages, such as math, art, and music.

They can include new terms they've learned, real-life uses, and math problems for their classmates to solve.

TIP

Slightly overlapping the photographs helps tie the elements together.

D Is for Drama

Students can devote an entire page to a single theme that begins with their letter.

Digital Cameras

Investing in an inexpensive digital camera allows you and your students to take photographs of activities throughout the year. Use photographs to personalize scrapbook pages.

Manipulatives

Adding manipulatives such as playbills and accordion books to the scrapbook page invites the reader to interact with the page.

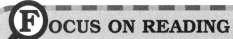

Mini-Reviews

Children can photocopy and color a cover of a favorite class novel and glue a review inside.

FOCUS ON READING

Brainstorm the ABC's of reading with your students. Encourage them to list titles of class novels, the parts of a book, genres, types of figurative language, literature awards and winners, and so on. Ask students to create banners for each letter to hang around the classroom to remind them of the many possibilities that reading provides.

The more you read, the more you know.
The more you know, the smarter you grow.
The smarter you grow, the stronger your voice,
When speaking your mind or making your choice.
—Anonymous

SCRAPBOOK BOOK REPORTS

Have your students experience a story through the eyes of the main character as they construct super-sized scrapbook pages from a character's point of view.

Winnie Foster, the main character in the popular novel *Tuck Everlasting*, "created" this scrapbook page, recording the magical week she spent with the Tuck family. It includes a synopsis of the story told in a diary entry, a letter to another character, and an advice column Q&A that explores the central problem of the novel.

Character Relationships

Students can explore relationships between different characters in the story by writing a letter from one character to another.

TIP

Computer-generated fonts can make titles clean and colorful. Gluing letters to squares of construction paper and tilting them on the page adds a playful effect.

Journaling

Writing is the most important part of scrapbook projects. Have students draft, edit, and carefully proofread their writing before copying it neatly into the scrapbooks.

Ask students to create a simple background that reflects the main setting of the novel by cutting out basic shapes from construction paper and gluing the shapes to the page. They can place their scrapbook elements on top of this background. Refer to page 24 for a suggested list of things students can include in their scrapbook book report.

Manipulatives

Manipulatives, such as this mini-book, encourage the viewer to explore the display in a tactile way. Follow the directions on page 65 to learn how to create a mini-book.

3-D Objects

Place 3-D objects in plastic bags, then attach with tape or glue.

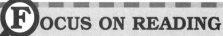

FOCUS ON READING

As students plan this scrapbook book report, help them improve their organizational and reading recall skills by asking them to keep a list of items the main character uses and the places the character visits throughout the course of the story. Students should add to this list after reading each chapter. When they finish the book, this list will help them recall important plot elements.

*Prose—words in their best order;
poetry—the best words in their best order.*
—Samuel Taylor Coleridge

OETRY SCRAPBOOKS & JOURNALS

Making poetry scrapbooks allows students to enjoy their work for years to come as they publish their own poems, reflect on inspiring verses by favorite poets, and record classroom poetry exercises.

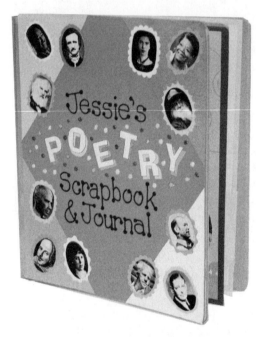

3-Ring Binders

Binders are great for poetry scrapbooks. They allow students to add pages throughout the year, and the pocket pages inside the front and back covers provide handy storage spots for works in progress.

TIP

Ask students to create a cover for their poetry scrapbook. The example above uses pictures of famous poets found on the Internet. The title was printed on the computer using an outline style. The letters were cut out with a piece of construction paper behind them and offset to produce colorful drop shadows.

Typographical Poems

Have students create a shape (or concrete) poem based on a family photograph. A photo of their family at the beach might feature a poem in the shape of a palm tree or wave; a garden photo could accompany a flower-shaped poem.

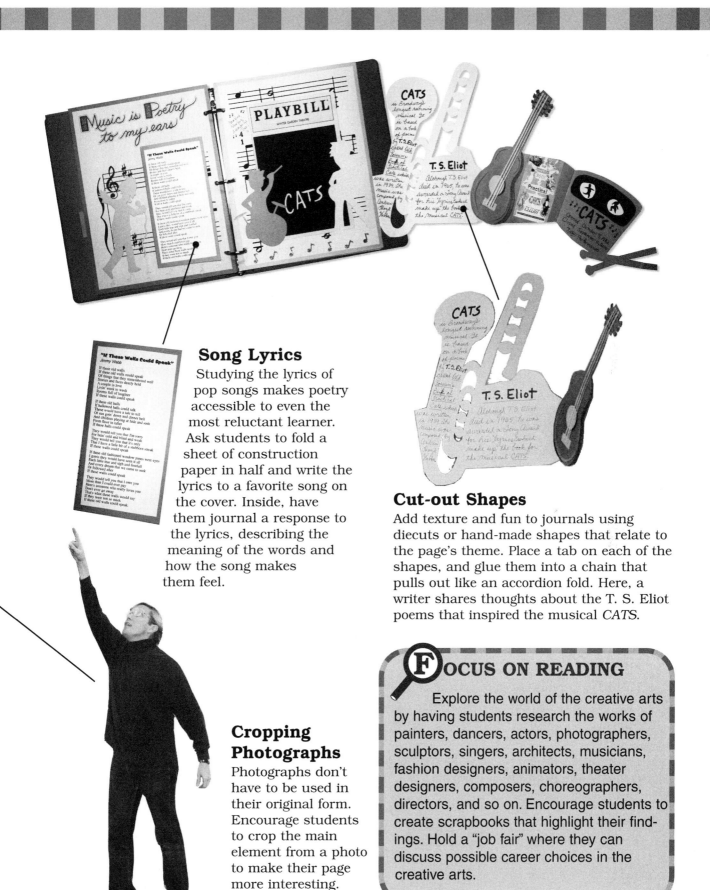

Song Lyrics

Studying the lyrics of pop songs makes poetry accessible to even the most reluctant learner. Ask students to fold a sheet of construction paper in half and write the lyrics to a favorite song on the cover. Inside, have them journal a response to the lyrics, describing the meaning of the words and how the song makes them feel.

Cut-out Shapes

Add texture and fun to journals using diecuts or hand-made shapes that relate to the page's theme. Place a tab on each of the shapes, and glue them into a chain that pulls out like an accordion fold. Here, a writer shares thoughts about the T. S. Eliot poems that inspired the musical *CATS*.

Cropping Photographs

Photographs don't have to be used in their original form. Encourage students to crop the main element from a photo to make their page more interesting.

FOCUS ON READING

Explore the world of the creative arts by having students research the works of painters, dancers, actors, photographers, sculptors, singers, architects, musicians, fashion designers, animators, theater designers, composers, choreographers, directors, and so on. Encourage students to create scrapbooks that highlight their findings. Hold a "job fair" where they can discuss possible career choices in the creative arts.

Colorful Poetry

Colors have long been associated with feelings and ideas—red signifies anger and yellow conveys cowardice. But what does yellow taste or look like? How does it smell or sound? How does it make you feel, and what does it feel like to the touch?

Collages

Students can glue their poems onto sheets of color-coordinated construction paper and surround them with a collage of stickers, hand-made accessories, and pictures clipped from magazines that feature the color mentioned in the poems.

Graphic Organizers

Give each student a copy of the graphic organizer on page 43. Ask them to write the name of a color in the top oval.
Under the headings of the five senses, students should brainstorm a list of things their chosen color might taste like, sound like, smell like, and so on. Students can use this list to help them write their poems. The graphic organizer can be added to their poetry journal alongside their finished poem.

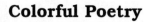

White is the color of an Arctic fox.
It's the lightest color in a crayon box.
It represents good in Old West flicks.
It's the smell of a bundle of aspen sticks.

Yellow is the color a coward feels.
Yellow is the flavor of banana peels.
It falls from the sky on a bright summer's day.
It's the center of daisies and the scent of hay.

GRAPHIC ORGANIZER

NAME: _____ **DATE:** _____

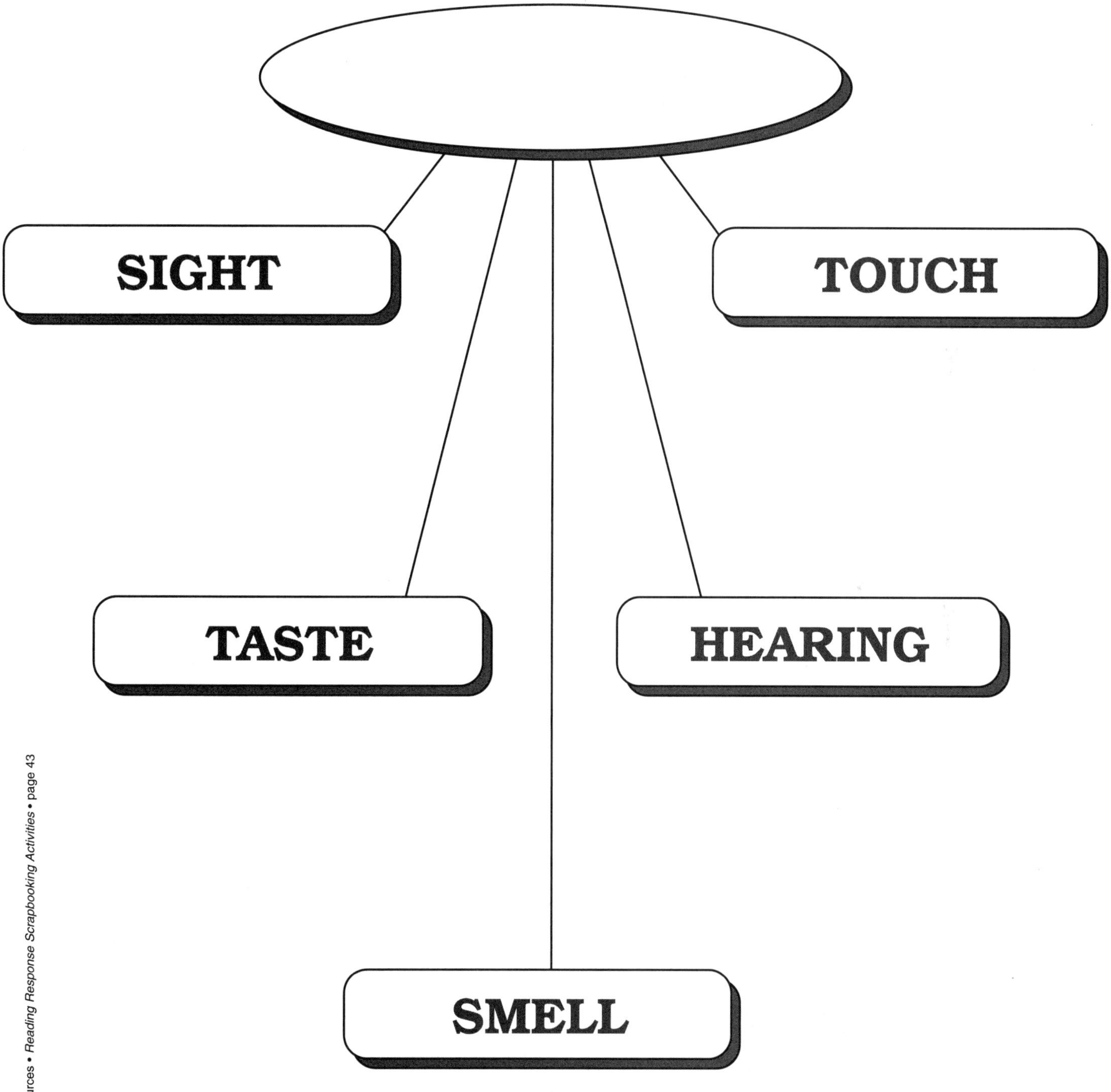

SIGHT

TOUCH

TASTE

HEARING

SMELL

I never know what I think about something until I read what I've written on it.
—William Faulkner

DAILY JOURNAL SCRAPBOOKS

Using a composition notebook, students can record their thoughts and feelings about their reading in a daily journal scrapbook. Have them include interesting objects and drawings on each page with their responses.

Cover
Have students personalize their Daily Journal Scrapbooks by decorating the covers.

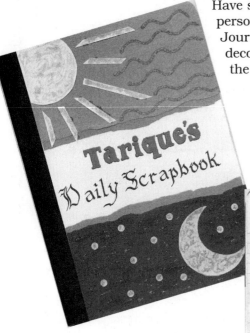

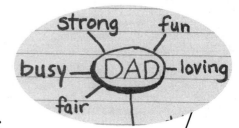

Grammar
Incorporate grammar into scrapbooking by asking students to list adjectives, nouns, and verbs that relate to a photograph or drawing.

Scanners
Scanners and copy machines allow you to reduce or enlarge programs, photographs, and drawings without harming the original.

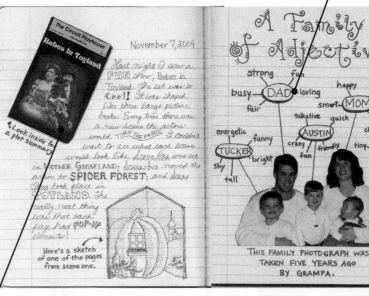

FOCUS ON READING
Use the list of reading response prompts on pages 45–46 for ideas. Extend the writing to other areas with the list of daily journal prompts on page 47. After assigning several of these, your students will get the hang of it and can then add their own personal reflections each day.

READING RESPONSE PROMPTS

Type of Prompt	Sample Prompt
Recall	- Summarize the chapter you just read. - Draw a picture of the climax of the story. - List five adjectives that describe the main characters in the book. - Describe the setting of the story. Illustrate it. - What is the major problem the main character faces? How is it solved?
Prediction	- How do you think the story will end? - Which character do you think will change the most by the end? How? - Who do you think the culprit is? - Based on the title of the book, what do you think the book is about? - Look at the illustrations. What do they tell you about the book? - Draw a picture of what you think will happen next. Describe it in a sentence.
Connections	- How is this book similar to another you have read by this author? - Which character is most like you? In what ways? - Create a Venn diagram that compares the setting of this story to the surroundings where you live. - How have you changed after reading this book? - What were your feelings after reading the first chapter of this book? - Draw and describe an event from your life that is like an event that happened in the story. - What advice would you give a character in this book? Why? - Which character would you most like to be? Why? - Which character makes you angry? Why? - Write an e-mail that you would like to send to the author. - If you were a character in this book, how would it affect the plot? - Compare a character in this book to a character from another book you read. - Describe a character's personality trait that you'd like to possess. Why do you like this trait?

READING RESPONSE PROMPTS

Type of Prompt	Sample Prompt
Opinion	- Why do you think the author chose the opening line he or she did? Do you like it? Did it make you want to read further? - Who is your favorite character? Why? Draw a picture of this character. - What do you think of the antagonist's actions? Are they right or wrong? Why? - What do you think is the most important scene in the book? - How would a different setting affect the story? - Was the cover design effective? Did it make you want to read the book? Create a cover design that you think readers would like. - Did you like the ending of the book? How would you have liked it to end? Rewrite a new ending for the book. - Write a question you would like to ask the author. How do you think he or she would respond?
Language	- Write five words that you find interesting or unfamiliar. Write their definitions and use them in a sentence. - Copy a sentence from the book that you think is well written. Why do you like this sentence? Illustrate it. - Find examples of figurative language in the text. Write them down. - What is your favorite line spoken by a character? Why do you like it?
Evaluation	- Did you enjoy the book? Why or why not? - Was the book hard or easy to read? Why? - What didn't you understand in the story? I'll respond to your questions when I check your log. - What do you know now that you didn't know before? - Describe your feelings after finishing the book. - Would boys and girls enjoy this book equally? Support your answer. - Would you like to read more books by this author? Why or why not? - Do you think the author chose a good title for the book? Why or why not? - What did you learn about the time in which the story took place?

DAILY JOURNAL IDEAS

- Write about your typical day. Include a sketch of a hobby you do most days.

- Glue a local weather report to the page. What do you like/dislike about today's weather?

- Glue a movie or theater ticket to the page. Write a review.

- Write the recipe of one of your favorite meals. Draw a picture of the meal.

- List five things that you are thankful for today. Include an icon for each.

- Glue a family photo to the page. Write five adjectives that describe each person shown.

- Draw a sketch of something that impressed you today. Write about it.

- Clip the title of your favorite magazine to the page. List ten things that you like about the publication.

- Find a leaf and make a rubbing of it. Print out a picture of the tree from the Internet and include it. Write some interesting facts about the tree.

- Who is your idol? Why? Attach a list of his or her accomplishments.

- Find a newspaper article that interests you. Attach it to the page and write a response that includes the "5 Ws and How." Use the graphic organizer on page 21.

- Tape a baby picture of yourself to the page. Ask your parents to tell you an interesting story about when you were little. Write the story in your journal.

- Make a handprint on the page. Become a fortune teller and write a story about what the future holds for you.

- Attach a timeline that shows each year you've been alive. Write a sentence for each year that highlights a major event.

- Draw a picture of a job you would enjoy performing. Describe the steps needed to become employed in that profession. What are the job's responsibilities?

- Write about an important person in your life. Include a drawing or photo.

- Draw a floorplan of your house. If you could have a special room in the house, what would it contain? Add it to the floorplan.

- Create a Top Ten list of your choice. Write about the number one selection.

- Interview a grandparent or older relative. Create a graphic organizer that compares similarities and differences between his or her childhood and your own.

- Find an outline of the United States and color in the states that you have visited. List things that you like about each state.

- Draw a picture of something you've done that makes you proud. Write about your accomplishment.

- Attach a cartoon that you think is especially funny. Sketch one of the characters and describe what you find humorous about the cartoon.

- Interview someone about his or her job and attach a business card.

- Write your favorite word and its definition, and then draw a picture that expresses the word. Explain why the word is your favorite.

- Attach a ticket from a sporting event that you attended. Write a descriptive paragraph about the competition using strong action verbs.

- Write a list of your goals. What do you hope to accomplish in the next week? The next month? The next year?

In a country as big as the United States,
you can find fifty examples of anything.
—Jeffery F. Chamberlain

TRI-FOLD STATE SCRAPBOOKS

Scrapbooks do not have to be confined to flat pages or posters. Open boxes with special objects inside, baskets, organizing trays, and tri-fold posters, such as the Tennessee scrapbook below, make fascinating free-standing displays!

Social studies projects especially lend themselves to a scrapbooking approach. You can have students research their city and home state. They can visit the state tourist bureau and request brochures, maps, and other free materials. They can also spend time at historical museums, as well as visit parks and monuments. When the unit is over, have students work in groups to create scrapbook displays that highlight their experiences and the information they learned.

State Quarters
Students can learn about state quarters at www.usmint.gov.

TIP

Use tracing paper and pencils to create rubbings of indigenous leaves, the bark from the state tree, or state quarters. Tape or glue the rubbings to the tri-fold scrapbook.

Postcard Template

Have students use this template to create a postcard that is written from the point of view of a tourist visiting the state featured on the tri-fold scrapbook. Students can design a stamp related to the state.

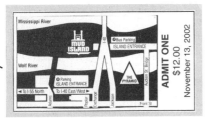

Souvenirs

Collect souvenirs such as tickets and postcards.

Pockets

Display brochures, letters, and other printed material in a pocket on the scrapbook page or poster.

FOCUS ON READING

The three sections of a tri-fold display are perfect for focusing on elements associated with the beginning, middle, and end of a story. Students can work individually or in groups of three to create a tri-fold display that sequences the main ideas from these parts of a novel.

SCRAPBOX COUNTRY REPORTS

Student archeologists will unearth a bounty of knowledge while creating chests filled with national treasures of a country and culture they research.

Ask students to bring a shoe box to class, which they will fill with objects and drawings that represent aspects of their chosen country's topography, culture, cuisine, economy, flora, fauna, government, sports, art forms, people, religion, history, traditional costumes, and ceremonies.

TIP

Use this same idea with other themes. A covered wagon could contain items that pioneers might have used, a treasure chest could highlight the life of a pirate, or a music box could feature mementos collected by a famous composer.

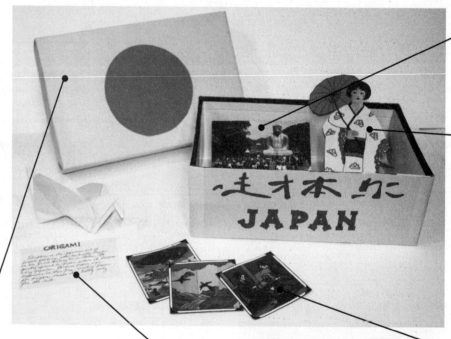

Country Flag

Use construction paper and markers to turn the lid of your shoe box into the country's flag.

Facts at a Glance

For each item in the box, write a paragraph on an index card that describes the object's significance.

Postcards

Although foreign postcards might be hard to find, the Internet allows students to create their own using photographs and images found on websites. A simple search using the country's name will provide students will many options. They can glue the picture to the front of the postcard template found on page 49.

TIP

Allow students to practice their public speaking skills. Ask them to give a short oral report on their selected country by opening the scrapbox, revealing each item to the class, and explaining its importance.

Costumes

Students can create a paper doll that wears the traditional costume of the country they're studying. Use the template on page 76.

Snapshots

Turn your students into photojournalists. Pass out copies of the snapshot template on page 71 and have students illustrate the sights, landforms, and architecture found in their chosen country. They can write notes on the back of each "photograph."

FOCUS ON READING

Scrapbox reports work well with fiction or nonfiction. Students can collect objects that a protagonist or antagonist might have picked up, or they can create the scrapbox of a U.S. president or a famous scientist.

The past is a foreign country; they do things differently there.
—Leslie Poles Hartley

A DECADE IN REVIEW

Each decade of America's past was filled with unique people, events, styles, and accomplishments. Create a classroom of student historians by having them work in cooperative groups to study important decades of America's past.

TIP

Cover several decades in a short period of time by dividing the class into groups that become "experts" in different decades of America's history. Each group will create a learning poster and then present its findings to the class in the form of a group oral report. Students can dress in the style of the decade their group researched by creating "clothing" out of paper bags, or they can create paper doll figures dressed in period costumes.

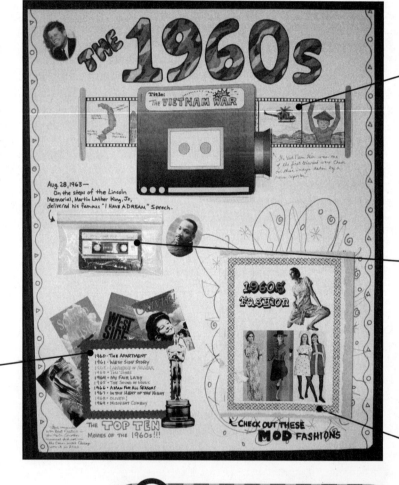

Top Ten Lists

Listing the top ten in a series—movies, books, inventions, cities, and so on—exposes the class to key elements and main ideas related to each decade.

FOCUS ON READING

Have each group read a story, picture book, or magazine that was written in the decade they're researching. Discuss ways in which writing styles and subject matter has changed in the last 100 years.

Scholastic Resources

Check out *35 Ready-to-Go Ways to Publish Students' Research & Writing* by Michael Gravois (Scholastic, 1998) for manipulative ideas that students can create, such as this video camera.

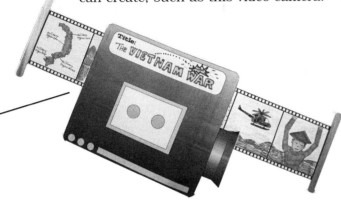

Aug. 28, 1963—
On the steps of the Lincoln Memorial, Martin Luther King, Jr., delivered his famous "I HAVE A DREAM" Speech.

Aural Learning

Listening to recordings of famous speeches and music from the era is a great way to transport the class to another time.

RESEARCH TOPICS

- people—politicians, artists, entertainers, scientists, authors, newsmakers, and so on
- inventions and discoveries
- major events and news
- fads, fashions, and hairstyles
- international relations and wars
- music, dance, theater, and art
- advancements in transportation
- significant events in economics
- major laws that were passed
- social advances
- women's roles
- civil rights
- natural disasters
- population shifts

Student-Made Magazines

Copy or download pictures and ads from magazines published during the decade you're researching to create a visual guide to fashions, fads, and hairstyles of the time.

DESK BLOTTERS OF FAMOUS PEOPLE

Students can learn about the deeds and accomplishments of significant people by imagining the types of things that might be found on their desktops—letters, awards, photographs, and important keepsakes.

Personal Items

Create three items that the person might place on his or her desktop. Write a sentence describing the significance of each item.

People Books

Follow the directions on page 72 to make a people book of the person you're researching. Write a couple of paragraphs that describe the person's major accomplishment.

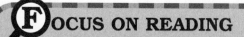

🔍 FOCUS ON READING

Instead of using a desk blotter as a background, have students create a scrapbook background related to a fictional character or real person from a book they are reading. Gene Autry might use a saddle bag; Harry Potter, a school bag; Florence Nightingale, a doctor's bag; and Mary Poppins, an oversized purse.

Timelines

Follow the directions at right to make an accordion book timeline of the person's life.

Snapshots

Use the snapshot template on page 71 to create "photographs" of major events in the person's life.

Use the snapshot template on page 71 to create "photographs" of major events in the person's life.

HOW TO

1. Cut a sheet of legal-sized copier paper in half vertically.

2. Tape the two lengths together.

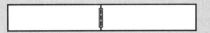

3. Fold the strip of paper accordion-style so you end up with eight panels. To do this, fold the long strip of paper in half three times and open it to reveal the eight panels. Use these folds as a guide to finish the accordion book.

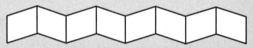

4. On each of the eight panels, write the date of a significant event in the life of the person. Write a couple of sentences describing the event and draw an icon representing it.

5. Write a title for your accordion book on the cover.

Amelia Earhart
#5 Place de Vege
Paris, France

George Putnam
555 Fifth Avenue
New York, NY

Language Arts

Incorporate the concept of first-person narrative by writing a letter in the voice of the famous person.

NIMAL HABITAT POSTERS

Educational scrapbook posters are a great way to get students excited about science. Working in cooperative groups, kids can design posters on topics that match your curriculum—from space to the human body to animal habitats. Stress that part of the final grade will be determined by how well the students share in the production of the final poster.

MUSKOX

Arctic Animals

The Internet is a wonderful resource for finding clip art, such as the animals and tracks shown here.

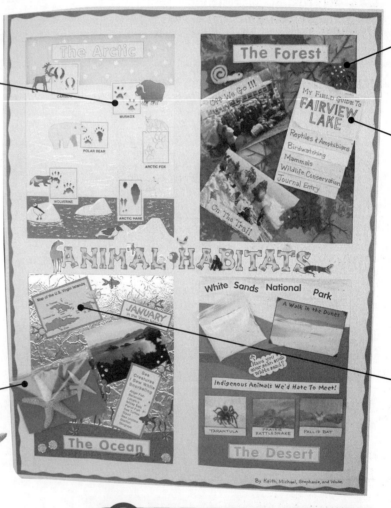

Starfish and Shells

Have students collect interesting and meaningful objects to add extra dimension to scrapbook posters. These items can be placed in a small plastic bag and then glued onto the poster.

FOCUS ON READING

There are dozens of science magazines for kids. Ask your librarian to subscribe to some of them so your class can use them as a resource.

Craft Spiders

Let your students use craft supplies and imagination to enliven their projects. This spider was made from colored pipecleaners and toothpicks.

Stencils and Stickers

Use stencils to create interesting titles for the posters. Animal stickers make this title even more playful. Ask students to bring in any stickers they might have to help decorate their projects.

My FIELD GUIDE To
FAIRVIEW
LAKE

Reptiles & Amphibians
Birdwatching
Mammals
Wildlife Conservation
Journal Entry

1. To create a flipbook, cut a sheet of paper into three panels.

2. Lay the panels on top of each other so that 3/4" strips of the back panels show at the bottom.

3. Bend the tops of the panels backward to reveal panels 4, 5, and 6. Fasten the top with two staples.

Forest Flipbooks

Have kids add individual projects to the group project in flipbook, mini-book, or letter form. Follow the directions above to create a flipbook.

Detail Maps

Scrapbook projects are a great opportunity for kids to work on their map skills.

TIP

Consider using unique papers and textures for the backgrounds of each section.
The Arctic—Tracing paper becomes a hazy, transparent sky.
The Forest—Silk leaves create a realistic forest floor, across which pipe-cleaner bugs crawl.
The Desert—Sandpaper gives the impression of textured sand dunes.
The Ocean—Tin foil shines like water.

The most exciting phrase to hear in science, the one that heralds new discoveries, is not "Eureka!" but "That's funny . . ."
—Isaac Asimov

CIENCE EXPERIMENT SCRAPBOOKS

Scrapbooking is an ideal way to study the various steps used in the scientific method. As your class conducts a science experiment, have students document their hypotheses, procedures, and findings on a scrapbook page.

Collages

Creating collages is a brainstorming technique that allows students to find a collection of objects that all relate to a specific topic. This garbage heap was made by overlapping clippings from magazines.

OCUS ON READING

Invite students to explore the worlds of science by asking each student to create a scientific scrapbook that focuses on a particular field. Encourage them to do Web searches and read trade books as they research their topics. Suggested topics include political science, natural science, earth science, social science, computer science, biology, chemistry, engineering, genetics, meteorology, geology, astronomy, mathematics, engineering, botany, agriculture, epidemiology, microbiology, archeology, paleontology, seismology, zoology, ecology, psychology, and volcanology.

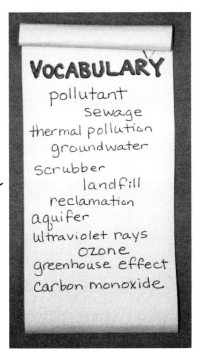

VOCABULARY

pollutant
sewage
thermal pollution
groundwater
scrubber
landfill
reclamation
aquifer
ultraviolet rays
ozone
greenhouse effect
carbon monoxide

Adding Dimension

Making objects more three-dimensional can add visual interest to the page. Simply curling the top and bottom edges of a piece of paper turns it into a scroll.

Data Disks

Use the templates on pages 73–74 and the directions below to create data disks that define and demonstrate the five steps of the scientific method. Review with students the steps below:

Step 1: Purpose—What do I want to learn?

Step 2: Hypothesis—What do I think will happen?

Step 3: Experiment—What test will confirm or disprove my hypothesis?

Step 4: Results—What happened during the experiment?

Step 5: Conclusion—What did I learn? Was the hypothesis correct?

Cross-Curricular Integration

Incorporate social studies into your science unit by having students report on different scientists who are involved in the field of study students are researching. Ask them to find out the steps one must take to become a scientist in that field and to discuss the job opportunities that are available.

HOW TO

1. Glue both data disks to a sheet of construction paper or posterboard. Cut out each template.
2. Cut out the viewing window on disk 1.
3. Place disk 1 on top of disk 2. Fasten the disks together by pushing a brass fastener through the black dot in the center of disk 1.
4. Add a title and illustration to the front of the data disk.
5. Write information about the five steps of the scientific method in the viewing window. Rotate the disk to write about each step.

Mathematics seems to endow one with something like a new sense.
—Charles R. Darwin

THE ART OF GEOMETRY

When creating a piece of art, artists often start with a foundation of geometric shapes, adding texture, color, and detail once they're pleased with the basic composition. Using the tangram, a geometry-based puzzle that people have enjoyed for centuries, students can develop an understanding of this technique. Ask them to create an imaginative scrapbook page that breaks images into their fundamental shapes.

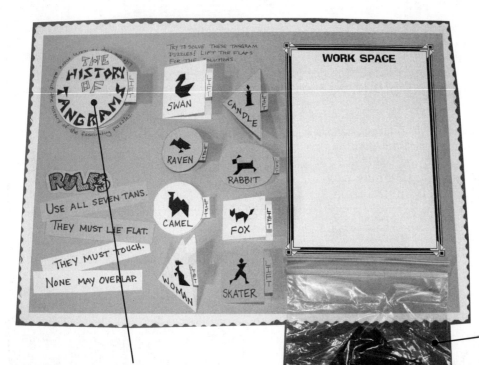

TIP

The Internet has hundreds of Web pages where you can find tangram puzzles. Challenge teams to solve them in timed contests!

Easy Access

Place tangram pieces in a self-sealing plastic bag, inviting the reader to create their own tangram puzzles. (Use the tangram template on page 61.)

Geometric Forms

Use geometric forms as the base of the elements on your page to create a bold composition. Shapes can feature a history of the tangram, vocabulary words, and silhouettes of tangram shapes.

FOCUS ON READING

Tangram games originated in China. Invite students to read about other Chinese games or games from various cultures. After learning the rules of these games, students can hold a *game fair*, in which they teach classmates how to play games from around the world.

TANGRAM TEMPLATE

NAME: _____ **DATE:** _____

Get the facts, or the facts will get you.
And when you get them, get them right, or they will get you wrong.
—Dr. Thomas Fuller

CRAPBOOKING GRAPHS & CHARTS

Instill in your students the importance of financial planning and investing by having them track and chart stock market prices over the course of ten weeks. They will also gain hands-on experience working with decimals, fractions, and graphs.

The stock market section of the newspaper makes an interesting, themed background for this page.

Adding Shadows

Water down black paint and use a small paintbrush to add shadows to the edges of objects to make them pop off the page.

OCUS ON READING

Have students read a section in their math textbook and create a scrapbook page that reflects its concepts. A unit on measurement can inspire a page about changing the classroom floorplan. A chapter on graphing can spark a comparison of class sizes throughout the school.

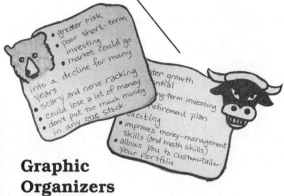

Graphic Organizers

Students can weigh the pros and cons of investing in the stock market by creating a graphic organizer.

Graphs

Students should create a graph that details the changes in each stock over the ten-week period or one that tracks the changes in their overall portfolio.

Charts

Have students make a conversion chart that lists fraction-to-decimal equivalents. They should create a second chart that shows the five stocks they "own," along with the corresponding stock symbols.

Porfolio Overview On Day One				
Stock Name	Stock Symbol	Number of shares	Price per share	Value of stock*
1. Dollar Tree	DllrTree	350	32.64	11,424
2. Pixar	Pixar	175	67.60	11,830
3. McDonalds	McDnlds	280	25.15	7,042
4. Time Warner	TimeWarn	500	18.40	9,200
5. WalMart	WallMart	200	52.40	10,480
			Total Portfolio Value:	$49,976

HOW TO

1. Divide the class into groups of four or five. Explain to students that each group will have $50,000 to invest in five different stocks, which they will track for ten weeks. Share copies of the stock market page, and point out that the column labeled "Last" (or "Close") lists the price for one share of that company's stock at the close of the day. This is the column with which they will be working.

2. Show students how to convert the fractional cost of each share of stock to a decimal. Demonstrate how they can multiply a fictional amount of shares by the decimal number to determine how much money the stock is worth. (For instance, if they own 50 shares of a stock priced at $38.125 per share, they own $1,906.25 worth of that stock.)

3. Groups should determine how much they want to spend on each stock, but they cannot spend more than $50,000 total. They should record the number of shares of stock they own in the five companies they picked and track the investments over the course of the next ten weeks.

4. On the same day each week, one student from each group should bring in the business section of the newspaper. Groups should then calculate the growth or decline in value of the five stocks they have selected and add the totals together. (They can use the Balance Sheet template on page 75.)

5. After the tenth week, students should create a scrapbook page that charts their stocks and the weekly changes in their portfolio.

Sports do not build character. They reveal it.
—John Wooden

THE WIDE WORLD OF SPORTS

Every culture is unique. Each has its own history, laws, costumes, political structure, and wars. Studying sports is much like studying cultures, each with its own history, rules, uniforms, and pecking order, with battles to be won and victories to be had. Tie physical education into your curriculum by having students create scrapbooks that focus on the various sports of the world.

Background

The playing field of the featured sport makes an ideal background for the scrapbook page. You could also visit a scrapbooking store and buy a piece of themed paper to use for the background.

Instant Replays

Use the snapshot template on page 71 to create "instant replay" photographs of great moments in the sport.

Timelines

Make an accordion-fold timeline that details the history of the sport (see directions on page 55). Accordion books can be cut like paper doll chains, hearts, flowers and so on. This timeline is shaped like a basketball.

Rule Books

Students can create rule books using the instructions at right. On the six interior panels, have students write some rules of the sport they're researching, including the number of players on a team. Ask them to illustrate the cover of the rule book.

Uniforms

Use the paper doll template on page 76 to create a sports figure dressed in the uniform of the sport he or she plays.

Themed Pockets

Themed pockets can hold a list of equipment used in the featured sport.

🔍 FOCUS ON READING

Use this scrapbooking activity as the catalyst for exploring other aspects of physical education: health and hygiene, the importance of exercise, proper diet, and so on.

HOW TO

1. Instruct students to fold a sheet of paper in half, as shown.

2. Have them fold it in half again in the same direction.

3. Then tell students to fold this long, narrow strip in half in the opposite direction.

4. Ask them to open up the paper to the Step 2 position and cut halfway down the vertical fold.

5. Students can open the paper and turn it horizontally. There should be a hole in the center where the cut was made.

6. Ask them to fold the paper in half length-wise.

7. Then show students how to push in on the ends of the paper so the slit opens up. They should push until the center panels meet.

8. Finally, have students fold the four pages into a mini-book and then crease the binding.

Every child is an artist.
The problem is how to remain an artist once he grows up.
—Pablo Picasso

EREAL BOX SCRAPBOOKS

Integrate the fine arts into your classroom by inviting students to create a cereal box scrapbook that focuses on a famous artist. By studying the life of the artist, students will learn that artistic expression comes in many forms and styles, artists come from a variety of backgrounds, and everyone has a unique creative ability.

Have students bring in a cereal box and cover it with construction paper or themed paper. The scrapbook elements can be glued to the outside of the box or placed inside.

Materials and Methods

Write a list of everything the artist needed to create his or her artwork. Under the list, write a paragraph that describes the method and style of painting the artist used.

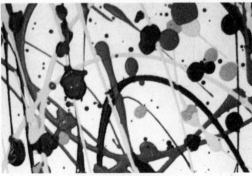

Reproduction

Reproduce an example of the artist's work. Student artists can learn a lot about artistic styles by copying the work of others.

Inside the Box

Students can place a variety of items inside the box that relate to the artist's life—copies of artwork, letters to the artist, photographs of the artist, significant items from his or her life, interviews, Internet research, and so on.

Responding to Artwork

Write a paragraph describing what you like about the artist's style and work. Think about the artist's color choices, subject matter, composition, and use of line, light, shape, texture, and shading.

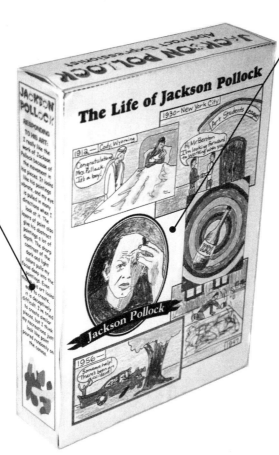

Comic Strip Biography

Use the template on page 77 to create a comic strip of the artist's life. Focus on the artist's early life, marriage, children, awards, education, major works, major artistic periods, and death.

BULLETIN BOARD SCRAPBOOKS

Turn a bulletin board into a super-sized scrapbook that emphasizes the learning that took place on a field trip. Because the bulletin board will feature work that is mostly created by the students, it not only saves you time, but it gives students a sense of ownership of the classroom by surrounding them with examples of their work. And best of all, it makes the space both educational and decorative.

Little Books

Little books are great to take on field trips. The books fit in students' pockets and provide just enough space for them to take notes and keep a record of things they saw and learned about. Follow the instructions on page 65 to make the little books.

T I P

Before going on a field trip, create a master template of the little book described at left. First, fold a blank sheet of paper into a little book. At the top of each panel write directions describing what you want students to record on each page. Vary the types of student responses to include lists, definitions, drawings, maps, descriptive paragraphs, webbing, and so on. Reopen the little book, and make a copy for each student. Then have students fold these templates into ready-to-go response vehicles that will keep them occupied and on task during the field trip.

Alphabetical Borders

Follow the instructions on page 36 to create an ABC list of things you learned and experienced on the field trip. Cut a length of bulletin board border into 26 strips. Each student can write a letter and phrase on the back of a strip. Surround your bulletin board scrapbook with these ABC strips.

Photographs

Take a camera with you on the field trip to record students in action and sights your class saw.

Found Items

Be on the lookout for field trip "freebies"—maps, brochures, postcards, playbills, tickets, shells, leaves, and so on. These add a lot of interest to the bulletin board when interspersed with student work.

TIP

Ask students to proofread their writing from right to left. This makes them focus on individual words. Otherwise, the brain tends to gloss over misspellings.

FOCUS ON READING

Read about field trips on the Web! Type the words "field trip" into a search engine and explore the many sites on this subject. Encourage your students to go on virtual field trips around the world!

INTEREST INVENTORY

NAME:_____ DATE:_____

Answer each question below and explain why you answered each question the way you did.

1. If you could be *anything* in the world when you grow up, what would you want to be?

_____

2. If you could travel any place in the world, where would you go?

_____

3. What is your favorite subject in school?

_____

4. What is your favorite hobby?

_____

5. What is your favorite TV show?

_____

6. What is your favorite movie of all time?

_____

7. What is your favorite animal?

_____

8. If you could be like any one great person, whom would you choose?

_____

9. If you were given $1,000, what would you do with it?

_____

10. Name five things that you think are your strongest assets.

_____

11. If you could change one thing about yourself, what would it be?

_____

12. Would you rather be very good looking, very talented, very smart, or very rich?

_____

13. What makes you happy?

_____

14. Name five things that you are thankful for.

_____

SNAPSHOT TEMPLATE

NAME: _____ **DATE:** _____

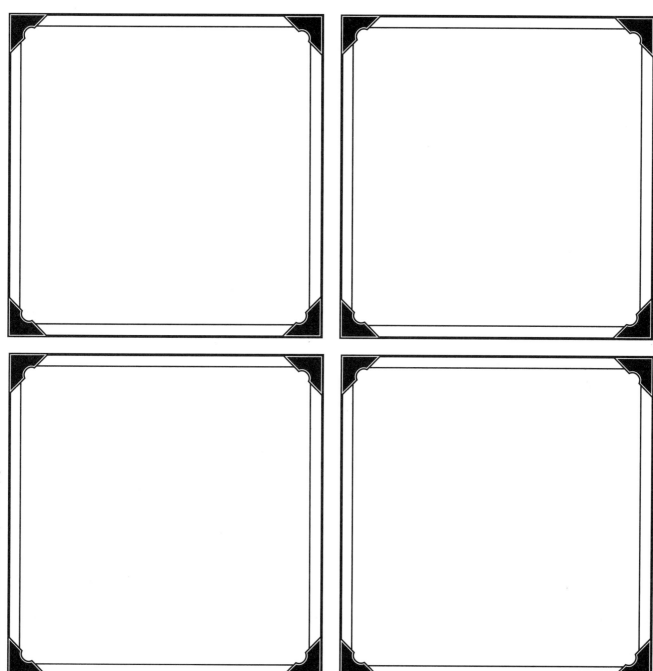

PEOPLE BOOKS TEMPLATE

FEMALES:

1. Fold a sheet of white construction paper in half twice horizontally and then once vertically.

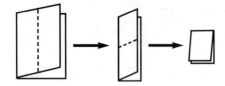

2. Open it up to reveal eight panels.

3. Cut the bottom left and bottom right panels along the dotted lines, as shown. Save the two scraps of paper.

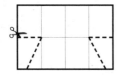

4. Next, fold in the top left and top right panels to create flaps.

5. Glue the two scraps from Step 3 behind the top two panels.

6. Add a head, legs, and hands to the figure.

7. Use buttons, markers, fabrics, dimensional glue, and other craft materials to decorate the figure. Create clothing that is representative of the person.

8. Use construction paper to create an object to put in the figure's hand that is relevant to her accomplishment.

9. Inside the two flaps, write two complete, detailed paragraphs describing the significance and the accomplishments of the person.

10. Finally, prepare an oral report on this person to give to the class.

MALES:

To create male people books, simply cut the bottom left and bottom right panels as indicated below, and make a slit up the center to create pants. Fold in the top panels (see Step 4), and glue the two scraps of paper that were cut away behind the top two panels to create sleeves. Then follow steps 6 through 10 above.

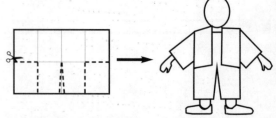

Scholastic Teaching Resources • Reading Response Scrapbooking Activities • page 72

DATA DISK TEMPLATE 1

NAME: _____ **DATE:** _____

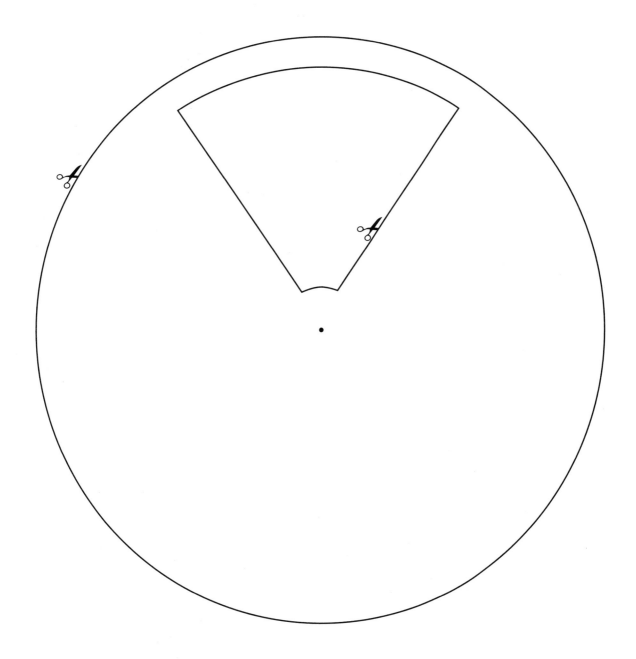

DATA DISK TEMPLATE 2

NAME: _____ **DATE:** _____

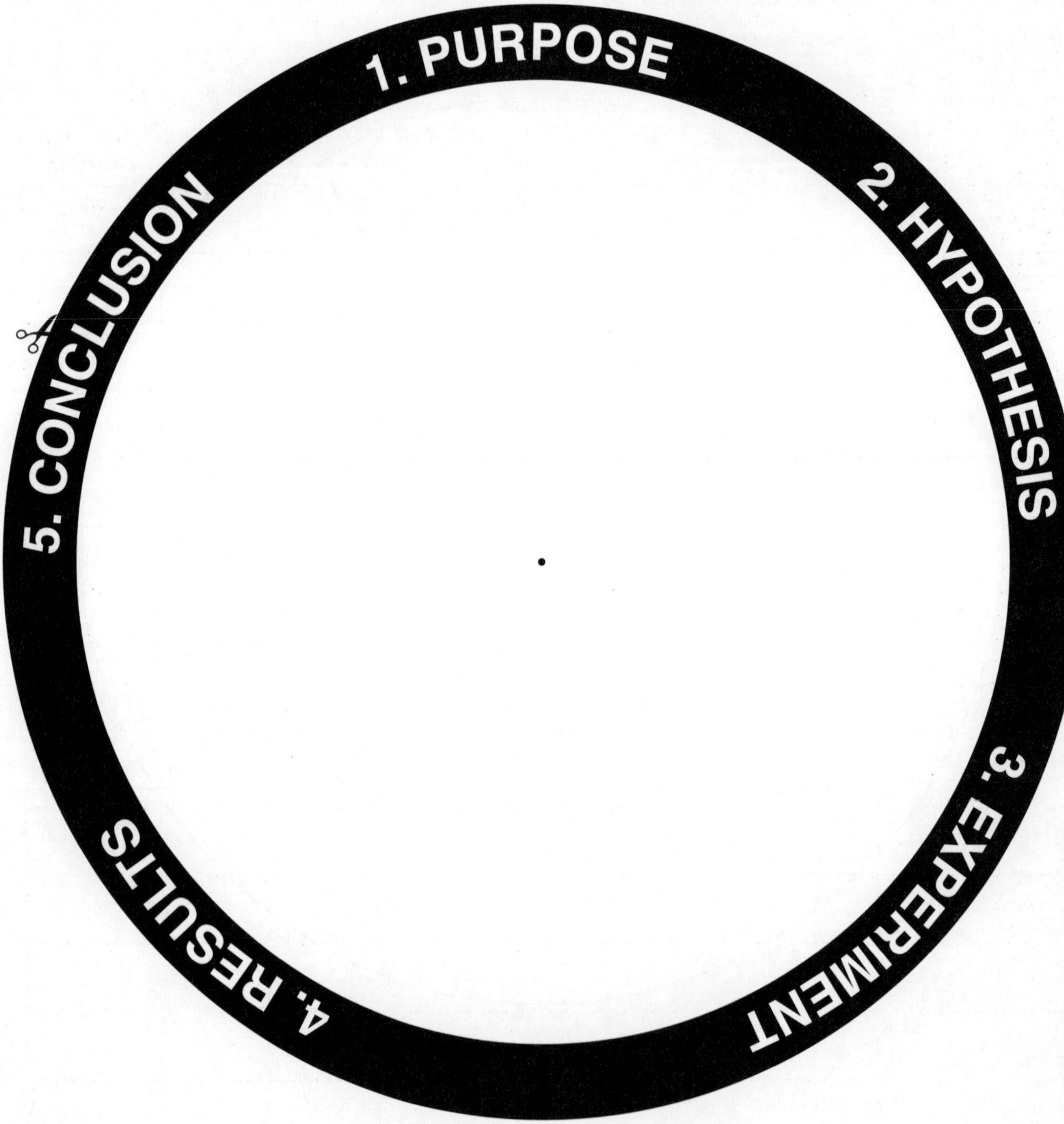

1. PURPOSE

2. HYPOTHESIS

3. EXPERIMENT

4. RESULTS

5. CONCLUSION

BALANCE SHEET TEMPLATE

NAME: _____ **DATE:** _____

Enter the information for each of the five stocks your group owns. Calculate the value of each stock and then add the totals together to find your total portfolio value.

GROUP: _____
WEEK: _____

Stock Name	Number of shares	Price per share	Value of stock*
1.			
2.			
3.			
4.			
5.			
Total Portfolio Value:			

* To calculate the value of your stock, multiply the number of shares you own by the price per share.

GROUP: _____
WEEK: _____

Stock Name	Number of shares	Price per share	Value of stock*
1.			
2.			
3.			
4.			
5.			
Total Portfolio Value:			

* To calculate the value of your stock, multiply the number of shares you own by the price per share.

PAPERDOLL TEMPLATE

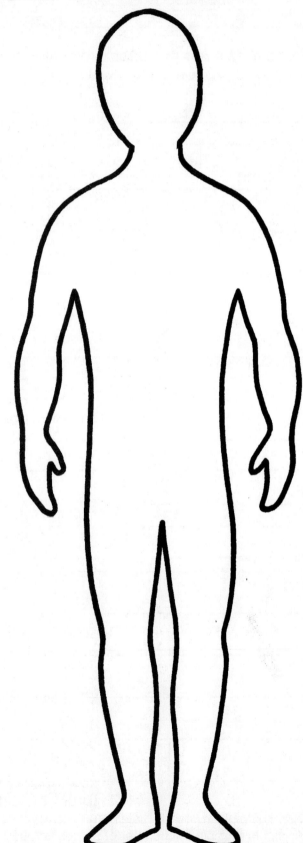

COMIC STRIP TEMPLATE

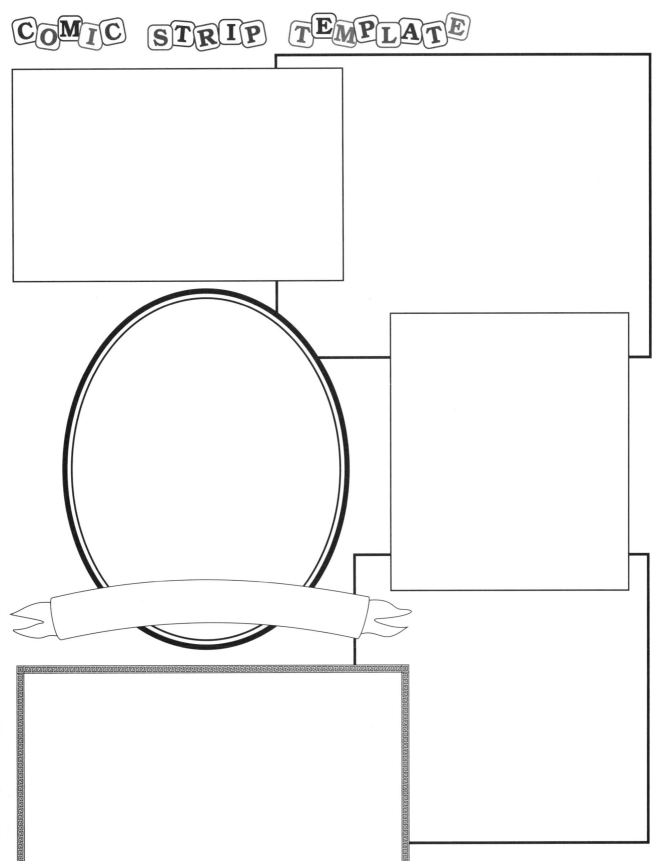

NAME: _____ **DATE:** _____

main character

two words describing character

three words describing setting

four words describing the main problem

five words describing an important event

six words describing an important event

seven words describing the solution

eight words describing the story's theme or moral

VENN DIAGRAM

NAME: _____ DATE: _____

Use this Venn diagram to compare and contrast two people, two characters, yourself and a character, and so on. Add hair and clothing to the figures.

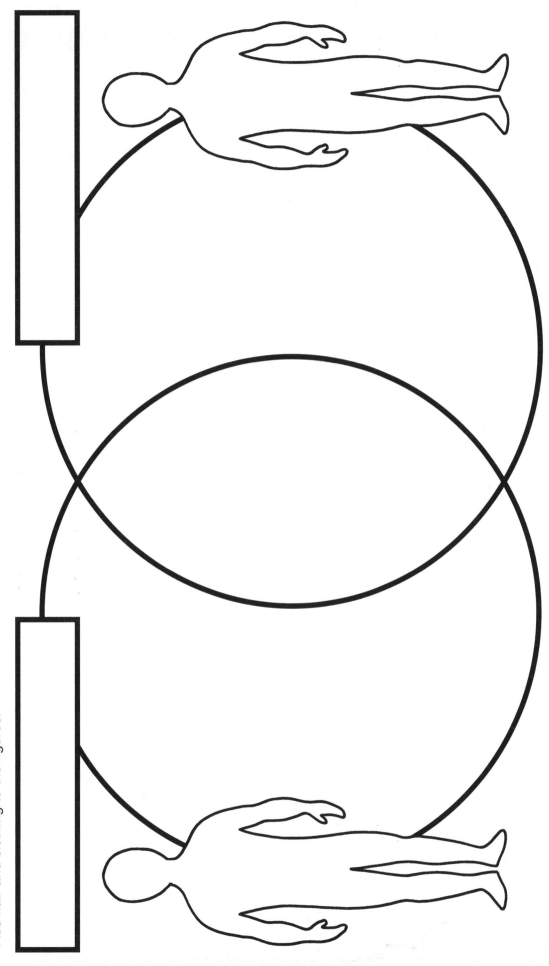

FIVE SENSES CHART

NAME: _____   DATE: _____

That makes sense to me! Think about a scene from the book. What does the character in that scene see? Hear? Smell? Taste? Touch or feel? Write your answers in the chart below. Use this information to help you create a scrapbook page about this character.

See	Hear	Smell	Taste	Touch

character's name